Grace

Marcia Lake

Copyright © Marcia Lake 2012

This edition published in 2013 by Hope Books.

Also available as an Amazon Kindle e-book for Kindle and i-technology.

ISBN-13: 978-1484186404

ISBN-10: 1484186400

Grace is typeset in Georgia Font and designed by
www.in-scribe.co.uk

For Isabelle, who is always with me.

Chapter One

Epsom

So... it all starts here, with a fantasy, with a dream.

There is a long dark tunnel and I'm walking through it. I'm in the lowest place I can be. I'm in a psychiatric ward. How did I get here? If there are cobwebs forming in my mind where did they start? I don't feel pain. I just feel numb.

I look around me and I'm in a dingy, dark, hell of a room where dusty, graffiti-ridden wallpaper is peeling off the walls.

The bed is rock hard, and I can hear loud, lunatic voices outside.

Welcome to Epsom Hospital!

What has happened before is all a blur. Somehow, I've been forced into an ambulance in Surrey and sectioned under the Mental Health Act. All I want to do is sleep, but there is a mass of voices in my head, and the voices all tell me different things. They provide a different story to my own reality.

I'll play dead.

I'll just lie here and pretend I'm not alive any more. But it's no good. I can hear my heart beating and the voices are so loud. I will tell you about them soon, but at the moment I need a rest.

There are words for people like me: lunatic, crazy, half-baked and yes, the most awful word of all schizophrenic". But, to myself, I am normal and I'm just experiencing a different kind of reality to the average person. I haven't harmed anybody, and I haven't harmed myself. I'm pretty sure that my doting parents will visit me shortly, smothering me with their enduring love. They are like strangers at the moment, but I still love them. I know that I am ill, but I can't admit this to anyone or to myself. I know that my mind is creating an escapist fantasy, in order to free itself of the grim realities of life. Right now, I just want to sleep, but I can't and I wouldn't trust a single person to be near me right now.

Someone knocks on the door. The door opens and it is my nurse. She has shiny, black skin and looks like Tracey Chapman.

'Maria, would you like to come and eat something? She says.

She calls me Maria because I have lied about my name.

'No thanks.' The last thing I can think of is eating right now.

'You really should try to eat something.'

'I don't want anything.' I reply bluntly.

Then, within a second, she is gone, and I've managed to push away another person.

Outside there is shouting, and then suddenly it calms down again. I slowly and bravely open the door, and there is a sort of Jack-the-Lad character, who is about 5'9 tall and a little bit chubby with blonde, flicked back hair and pale skin.

'You won't be in here for long, you know.'

My heart skips a beat. How does this man know anything about my situation? His kind words calm me, although it's obvious he's another patient. I suddenly become aware of the dark glasses I'm wearing. I feel a little daft wearing them indoors, but I have a vague idea they are protecting me from something. Maybe it's from the medical staff. I close the door quietly and take a deep breath. I need to get out of this place somehow and so I try to think of a plan. Suddenly, a flash of inspiration dawns on me.

I open the door slowly, and see the same Jack-the-Lad standing there. I say shyly:

'If I give you £5.00, could I borrow a mobile phone from you?'

Yes it's amazing. Somehow I have managed to bring a £5 note into Epsom Hospital with me.

'I don't have a mobile with me, but I can take your £5 anyway!' He says cheekily.

'No way,' I bluntly reply. I need to close the door now and let Jack-the-Lad disappear from my sight. My plan 'A' has gone out of the window.

It's getting dark. Shadows are dancing on the ceiling, and a leaky tap is making a monotonous sound. The odour coming from my body is not very pleasant. There is commotion outside. I can hear a girl screaming, and it sounds like she is being forcibly injected. It is upsetting to hear it. I must get a sense of who I am right now.

I'm Marcia and I've been sectioned under the 1983 Mental Health Act. I'm now an official statistic. I lie in my bed and think about how to get out of here. Right now though, I just want to sleep, so I close my eyes and drift off for a while, and my voices go to sleep with me.

Then I wake up suddenly, as a young lady with blonde hair, who looks like an angel, asks:

'Are you okay? Do you need anything?'

'No, I'm okay, thanks.'

She looks genuinely concerned for me, and, because of her kindness, she makes my hard, stoic face break into a half smile.

Then she shuts the door gently, but firmly. I open the bedside cabinet. Inside is a red, embroidered book with my conspiracy theory.

In capital letters is written: "I am Maria Lynch, daughter of David Lynch. I'm 19 years old and I've been abducted and brought to England. The people who claim to be my parents are not my real parents."

At the back of my mind, I know none of this is true. But the voices are telling me these things so convincingly, that it's hard not to believe them. I place the red book in the drawer and drift off with my voices.

I wake up startled, after an unpleasant dream. It's about my old Eurythmy teacher and he's walking down a spiral staircase - just about to give me medication. I guess you could call it prophetic. I have a fear of medication. I'm scared of what it might do to my major organs, but, for some reason, they have not given me any medication yet.

I drift off into the night, and a desolate feeling weighs on my heart. I have nobody but this voice, which I know is not real. It's the voice of Bono. Yes, it is Bono's voice.

Bono says he's going to come and get me and everything will be all right. Some people hear unpleasant voices - I have rock star talking to me! There's Edge too, with his strong, Irish accent - as clear as anything. They are giving me hope and I drift off to sleep again.

While I sleep, the high security psychiatric ward sleeps with me in the Borough of Surrey. It is situated just 18 miles south west of Charing Cross. At one time there were many psychiatric hospitals in Epsom, but they were closed down, one-by-one. The one I'm in now is the only one left.

To be asleep is better than coping with the underlying reality of where I have ended up. I believe in the existence of angels so I'm sad they have somehow eluded me.

The night goes very quickly and before I know it, its morning. I wake up to the sound of a knock on the door. It's Tracey Chapman again.

'Maria, it's time to have a shower and come down for breakfast.'

'Okay, but please leave me alone.'

There is something really annoying about Tracey. She's always in my space. She shuts the door and I shower. The white ceramic tiles are covered in dust and it is like having a shower in a prison cell. I wash my hair thoroughly, and, as the water falls down on my head, the voices retreat for a while. Then I get dressed and Tracey knocks again.

She gets a small towel and starts towel drying my hair roughly, and I have to pull back or my hair will go static.

'I'm okay. Please leave me alone.'

'Your breakfast is outside.'

But I have no appetite, especially when I see what they have served up! There is stale toast and a half-poached egg.

I am lying down again when the voices start. There is one particular voice that is prominent. She is called Roxanna and she is the head teacher of the Steiner College that I used to work at, before I got ill. She is going on and on at me; telling me she is my twin and she can help me get out of here. The voice is so demanding and loud that I am developing a headache. I tell her to "fuck off" but it just makes her stronger. Then there is a knock at the door.

A lady introduces herself as a doctor. She is Indian with sleek, black hair that is pulled back into a ponytail. She has pressed black trousers on, and a blue, shiny blouse. She looks very official.

'How are you?' She says.

'I'm fine. Please can I go home?' I say, angrily.

You can't go home yet. You need to get well first.'

She has a very authoritative way about her. I think I just don't stand a chance arguing with her.

Suddenly, I remember that I have some photos of myself, but I'm convinced they are not *me*. I think I can persuade her that I'm not ill; there is a conspiracy going on.

'Please look at these photos. It isn't me in these photos.' I say confidently.

'I deal with these sorts of cases every day and very rarely is there anything in it. The photos look like you.' She shrugs, like I am a nuisance to her.

It is like a punch to my lower abdomen. I so much want to be listened to and understood. I find her cold and without compassion.

'I just want to go home. I'm not taking medication of any sort.' I say triumphantly. But she answers sternly:

'If you refuse to take medication we will forcibly inject you.'

I grimace. I didn't know they had the right to do that. I thought you had to be violent and aggressive like the patients in *One Flew Over The Cuckoo's Nest*.

A tear comes to my left eye. I feel so vulnerable. The doctor leaves without a word of sympathy and the door slams behind her. I feel like I am dying. I feel like I have no control over my mind, and it is now in the hands of other people. I quietly sob.

The hours pass and I draw colourful shapes on plain pieces of paper. How I'd love to have a stereo and listen to U2. I lie down in the bed - it is about 3 p.m. on a foggy, December day. As I look out of the window, I can see the glistening grass, and behind that there is a metallic building. A woman stares at me through the window whilst I try to sleep.

Suddenly, in waltz the people who think they are my parents. I don't want to see them, so I pretend to be asleep. They keep saying my name: "Marcia". They stroke my back tenderly and my dad kisses my forehead. It is an ordeal to ignore them, because I need so much love at the moment, but I'm in no fit state to receive love.

I continue to ignore them and, after ten minutes, they give up and leave me. I have a strange feeling that they know I'm pretending to be asleep and I feel guilty. So what do I do now? I think of David Lynch who is my "imaginary father". He is talking to me and angrily condoning the people who have put me here. In my mind's eye I can see his handsome face, and it makes me think of why I am living in his world right now. Then the psyche comes to the surface and I'm experiencing the world of David Lynch inside this psychiatric ward. There are no severed ears or dancing dwarfs, but there are people experiencing pain and frustration. I was always undecided as to whether I liked *Eraserhead* or *Blue Velvet,* but now I've changed my mind. David Lynch is a strange man. He drinks ten cups of coffee a day, but still manages to do Transcendental Meditation. Maybe I should try that. But, for now, I am just happy to have him as my imaginary father. Apparently, David Lynch began meditating on the set of his first film *Eraserhead.* He loves to talk about it and he recently said:

"Meditation is beautiful. Happiness lies within. Enlightenment is our birthright."

Maybe one day when this is all over I can reach enlightenment, but not right now as the day is dragging on and I've decided to take a stroll up the corridor. I have my dark glasses on as I walk and there again is Jack the Lad. He says:

'You're very beautiful, will you marry me?'

That is sweet, but it makes me blush and I go back to my room. I decide to write out the lyrics of *The Joshua Tree,* as I have to do something to occupy my mind. The day goes slowly. Food is left outside my door and *Tracey* is nowhere to be seen. I eat pea soup and bread. I am so hungry. Another nurse knocks on my door and comes in.

'Hello Marcia.'

I don't like the look of her. She looks like a History teacher!

'Can I go home soon?' I blurt out.

'No you can't. You've been sectioned. You have to take medication and get better!'

This information drains my spirits. I don't want to hear anything more about medication.

I talk to my voices for hours after this. They reassure me that everything will be all right and I won't be here for long. Night draws in and there is a man at my door. He is friendly enough and obviously works here, so I decide to trust him. He is Asian and of slim build. I try to explain to him that I was part of a cult called "Anthroposophy", and it's all a big mistake. There is nothing wrong with me. This doesn't work and he tells me to take a tablet. When I refuse, he gets a little aggressive and I throw it in my mouth. Then he walks away, enjoying his victory over me. It is only then that I notice the tablet has fallen down the sink and I have victory after all! It's all part of some divine plan I think! So I go to sleep and slip in and out of consciousness.

Before I know it, the Manager of Epsom Hospital is at my door telling me they are going to move me to Rose Ward in Horsham, to be nearer to my mother. I am so happy about this. I'm sure Bono is waiting for me there. It's so late, but I pack the spartan belongings I have with me: a slip, a book, two U2 CDs and my purse. Would the place I am going to be any better? Will the Press be waiting for me there?

I'm sandwiched in the middle of an old *Vauxhall* car, between two nurses and god do I feel spaced out! Morrissey joins me in the car for the journey. I can hear his thick, Northern accent reassuring me. Something inside of me knows that I am going to a better place. I can feel the light above my head and it is far stronger then the voices.

I arrive at Rose Ward, and the place is very familiar. I'm in Horsham, not far from home. Again, the light dances above my head, and the voices diminish for a moment. I take a deep breath and climb the stairs to the hospital, and instantly this place is not so intimidating. I am ready for the next stage in my journey.

Chapter Two

Rose Ward

Rose Ward has 28 beds and provides psychiatric services to residents in Crawley, Horsham and the surrounding areas. There are two sections: a general adult psychiatric ward, and a separate ward for elderly mentally ill patients.

I am introduced to a nurse and I walk down a long corridor with beige walls and a dark blue carpet. I see two sets of dormitories to my right and beyond those are individual patient rooms.

I sit down inside a box-shaped room and feel a little intimidated, because the nurse has a clipboard in her hands. She asks me what my name is. I tell her and she compliments me on knowing my real name. I find this quite strange! Then she asks:

'Do you hear voices?'

Of course I reply "No". My voices are my secret and hopefully they will help me to get out of here soon.

'We will be putting you on medication to help ease your symptoms.'

This is not what I want to hear!

'What does the medication do?' I say, flatly.

'It will help to improve your mood – you'll feel better too.'

I remain silent. She is a gentle soul; a small, Indian lady and I don't feel threatened by her.

'I will show you to your room now,' she says.

There it is. My own room, which looks luxurious, compared to one at Epsom. There is a comfortable bed, a pine bedside cabinet, and a clean sink. The heating is on full blast and I don't mind it much really. I'm left alone for ten minutes, until a friendly black man knocks on my door.

'Your family has left you some things - come with me.'

I go to the office and see staff with badges around their necks, designed to make them look important. There are several bags on the floor, together with a CD player, some bottles of *Evian* water and packets of kettle chips. I'm so happy about this. I conclude that my mother has brought these things for me. I take everything to my room and drink nearly half a bottle of *Evian,* as I am so dehydrated. Most important of all is the CD player. We just go on with our everyday lives, taking such things for granted. I put on *The Unforgettable Fire* and the music blares out from the speaker. I'm in sheer ecstasy as I take in the music. There is only one thing to do now, and that is to write to Bono himself! But I'm not in a good state of mind. I still believe in the conspiracy: my parents are not my real parents etc. I'm sure that Bono will save me.

Dear Bono,

I'm in Rose Ward in Horsham and I've been sectioned. Please come and get me out of here at once. You are my true love and I know that you can save me. I want to come to Ireland and be with you. Please phone me. Thank you.

Love Maria.

I place the letter under my pillow. I will sleep with these words tonight and everything will be all right. It has to be! It has to! I'm relying on the Alpha man to not let me down.

Suddenly, a Chris Eubank look-a-like knocks on my door and says:

'50-50, phone a friend, or ask the audience! Dinner is ready!'

This cheers me up a little.

'I'll have it in here, please.'

Then, before I know it, fish and chips are left outside my door, and I eat it very quickly, as I am starving. Maybe I will even get away with not taking medication in this nice place! Well I can hope anyway. I put on another U2 CD, and the song *Bad* blares out from the speaker. It seems to sum up everything I feel at the moment.

My whole evening is spent listening to U2, even though I only have two of their albums with me and... I talk to my voices. Edge has got loud lately. He's a welcome change to Bono.

Suddenly it's night time and the jolly guy is at my door again.

'Medication time,' he says, methodically.

By now I'm exhausted and not prepared to argue, so I line up with the others. I have a fear of taking medication, so this is not easy for me. I place the container in my hand and swallow the wafer-like preparation. It dissolves on my tongue and isn't pleasant. I believe it could be poisonous, so I drink a whole bottle of *Evian*. I feel sedated and fall into a deep sleep. It is my first deep sleep in a long time. While I'm asleep, the effects of the drug take place, increasing my blood sugar, but sorting out my brain.

It's amazing how quiet it is here at night. You can hardly hear a pin drop.

When morning comes, I realise that I have heavily overslept. Then the nurse knocks on my door.

'Hello, Marcia, time to get up.'

The sedation carries on. I knew that the medication would have this effect.

The day goes on sluggishly until about 2 p.m. when my mother turns up with my brother. I shout at them to go away and they are gone. Again, I'm left alone but not for long as the nurse comes to my door.

'The doctor would like to see you now.'

I walk past the two dormitory sections and I'm guided to a door. Inside there are 6 or 7 people in a semi-circle, waiting to talk to me.

'Hello, Marcia, I'm the doctor.'

It is all so intimidating and I walk out, then go back to my room. When I'm there I burst into tears. I feel so alone and misunderstood. Night falls quickly and cruelly. I line up for my medication, than go straight to sleep.

The next day, nothing at all happens, until my mother visits. I'm still hearing voices, but my communication with people has started to improve. I'm just more rested.

'Can you get me the album: *All That You Can't Leave Behind*?'

I'm still obsessed with U2! I can't get enough of them!

'You look better today!' Mum says. She's started to become mum again!

'Why are you not at work?'

'I'm off this week and I've brought you a book of poems.'

'Thank you. Are you coming tomorrow?'

'Yes. I can do.'

She has done something special. She has given me a book of poetry. I start to read it and it calms my mind:

The Angel that presided o'er my birth
Said, 'little creature, form'd of Joy and Mirth,
'Go love without the help of any Thing on Earth.'
William Blake.

Then I decide that's what I want to do in here. I want to read and write poetry and, for the next week, this is all I do.

I have become obsessed, but my voices start to become less powerful.

My mum visits every day and I read out poetry to her.

Suddenly, a week has gone by and I'm due to see the doctor again. I sit down on the hard seat with 5 people all glaring at me.

'So, Marcia, how do you feel?' asks the doctor.

'I feel great.'

It is true. I am starting to feel better.

'That's the medication.'

I swallow hard. I don't want to hear that.

'You may have to take it for years.'

The doctor is Indian, and has a bald head and an *uncle* sort of way about him. He is kind, but I don't like what he is saying.

'The nurses tell me that you are doing a lot of writing. What are you writing?'

'Poetry.' I reply.

'Can we read some of it?'

I blush. I can't believe the doctor wants read my poetry!

'Okay, I'll go and get some.'

My room is at the end of the long corridor, and I look through the book, tearing out crazy poems. I run back down the corridor, eagerly giving the book of poems to the doctor. They all start reading my poems and a plump lady smiles, after reading one.

The doctor concludes:

'There is nothing dangerous in this. It is just good poetry. I have decided to give you one night's leave.'

I can't believe it. I can go home for one night, which means that I will definitely be able to post a letter to Bono.

The meeting comes to a conclusion. Then I realise that my dad is outside. He kisses my cheek. It's nice to see him. I get my things ready and I go to his car.

I want to cry from relief. Being locked inside a psychiatric ward is not pleasant. You can become institutionalised.

I see my dad's bright green BMW, and it's lovely to feel the leather seat beneath my bottom. He takes me to my mum's house in Theydon Close. I still hear voices, but they are less bossy; not so much in control. My dad leaves quite soon afterwards, and I have a cup of coffee with my mother.

I pick up *The Guardian* and I read quite an interesting article about the treatment of the mentally ill. Here are some things I find out:

"According to the charity Mind, some patients using mental health services are treated inhumanely and with a lack of respect. Face down restraint is often used too much, and they urge an end to it. We should not as a society be leaving people with urgent mental health needs isolated, frightened and unsupported in impersonal, hospital settings. We should not be traumatising those who use these services, to an extent that they would do anything not to return."

The article shocks me. I had felt a lack of respect at Epsom but I found Rose Ward quite respectful. I think it's very hard to deal with those experiencing mental distress and the question of Sectioning is controversial. I was not a threat to others, but I definitely was a threat to myself. I remember, before Epsom, how I had walked for miles in the pouring rain with the police looking for me. An Irish man I did not know started to talk to me in my head and told me that I could walk from Crawley to my dad's shop in Dormansland, which was 25 miles away. The rain was falling so hard that I got a severe cold and a cough that was so bad, I started to choke. So, yes, sometimes there's no other way then to be sectioned.

I feel like I've stepped out of prison.

I observe my purple and green bedroom with its chest of drawers and rocking chair in the corner. It's a little girl's room. Even though I'm feeling better, I still feel like a little girl.

I have chicken pie and chips with mum, and then I settle down to watch a little TV in the evening. After that, I retreat to my room with an important mission in mind. I need to write to Bono again. These letters are therapeutic and are aiding my recovery:

Dear Bono,
I'm now taking medication, and I will probably be home soon. You are my true love and I want so much to meet you and the band. I can't understand why you are not replying to my letters. I agree to see a psychiatrist when I come over to Ireland.

Somewhere, in the back of my mind, a light shimmers and that light tells me not to believe in the unbelievable. No rock star can reply to you. Even if he wanted to, he probably receives thousands of letters every month and it's just impossible. But writing is a form of healing to me and until I think about how I'm going to rebuild my life, I have to focus on something. So letters it is.

I play *Heartland*. This song holds a special meaning for me. Then, for some reason, I think of Carl Jung. He was such an influential thinker in his time. It's a shame he can't be my psychiatrist. I think about the process of *individuation* and how it leads us to becoming whole. In *Psychological Types* I recognise myself as the introverted intuitive type, who is often an artist and mystical dreamer. He believed that therapy could restore and heal a broken psyche. Anything is possible I guess.

I look at my mother. She is tired and I'm probably to blame for that. She visits me nearly every day and has to listen to me talking about nonsense and humming away to U2. Daughters aren't always easy to cope with.

It is like someone has put a black leather jacket over my eyes tonight. I am out for the count. I wake up at 7 a.m. and jog to the post box to mail my letter.

The light doesn't stop shimmering: *You will find your way home.*

It knows I'm not going to meet Bono right now.

The next day, I return to Rose Ward - my dad takes me back. He gets into a huge argument with the nurse because they have moved me to the dormitory. I don't even have my own room now. My dad looks so sad about leaving me there. He kisses my forehead and I'm left alone. Next to me is Rita who is small and has white hair and piercing blue eyes. She shakes my hand and says things like: "The light is burning my skin" and "The medication makes me forget".

I walk down the corridor and see a stack of magazines piled on top of each other. I open one and see a picture of Bono performing, looking gorgeous. I have it at the side of my bed as I go to sleep but, alas, when I wake up in the morning, it is gone.

Chapter Three

Eurythmy

Eurythmy is an expressive movement of art originated by Rudolf Steiner, in conjunction with Marie von Sivers, in the early 20th century. Primarily a performance art, it is also used in education, especially in Waldorf schools and as a movement therapy. The word eurythmy stems from the Greek, meaning beautiful or harmonious rhythm.

Christmas, 2004 is a tricky one.

The days pass by and my voices lose their grip on me and, before I know it, I am discharged from Rose Ward. I haven't made one single friend there and I don't have any friends at all.

I live with my mum in the same house that I grew up in.

A community psychiatric nurse visits my home; she is Northern and plump, with grey eyes. I find her quite annoying.

'I really think you should read about your condition, and try to understand it.'

'Why do I need to do that?' I say, bluntly.

'It will help you to come to terms with it. What about friends and boyfriends?'

I just shrug. I have no friends and no boyfriend.

'So, let's try and plan your week. Do something every day.' She says.

'I could go for a walk round Tilgate Park.'

'That would be good. There is also Art Therapy available, if you would like to do that - but you really must be willing to open up to it.'

'Yes, I think that will help me.'

We have these meetings in my beautiful living room, which my mum designed so well. There are sculptures on shelves and two Kandinsky paintings on the walls. But I am a little down. There is no direction to my life now. I miss performing Eurythmy and teaching it to children. I miss visible speech and visible music. I remember the sounds and rhythms of speech and the tones and rhythms of music and how my body felt like electricity when I moved. It was like there was a current running through me. I miss the curves and straight lines, the copper balls and the rod exercises. I loved the difference in mood between the major and minor pieces. But what had I done when I was becoming ill? I'd thrown all the choreography away, along with photos, medals and certificates. In contrast to the lean dancer I was, I am now twelve and a half stone, and I have to take a nap in the daytime, because of the medication. My CPN warned me that people on Olanzapine tend to stay at home and get fat, which was happening to me.

One day, out of the blue, I got a phone call from Hikari.

'How are you, Marcia?'

'I'm fine. Thanks for calling.'

'Are you on medication?'

'Not at the moment.' I lie, as I'm ashamed.

'There is a Eurythmy performance on Saturday. Would you like to come and see it?'

'Yes, okay.'

20

'We can meet at the Steiner College at 7 p.m.?'

'Yes, see you then.'

This is my chance I think. Hikari is still in the stage group, and might be able to get me back in there. But a memory starts to disturb me. I had sent silly letters to my teacher asking him to visit me in Rose Ward, and also to Anna and Debbie. It is obvious to everyone that I've had a nervous breakdown. How would they react to me now, after I had told the group that I didn't want to do the "fairy tale" any more, when, in fact, I was suffering from paranoid delusions that I was being set up.

So, on Saturday, I make my way by train to Victoria and catch the Tube to Baker Street. I am panicking, as a memory plays in my mind. It is my old Eurythmy teacher, during 4th Year - I am on stage. I dance to a Clemanti piece, but I'm not doing so well, as I can't remember the tones and where my arms should go. Eve dominates the front and I feel bewildered. I sit down and the next group goes on. I get in a really bad mood, because it isn't correct. When the teacher tells me to go back on stage I say:

'I'm not going.'

'Yes, you are. Go on stage now.'

The truth is, I feel ill and spaced out, and I know I am getting into a control drama with him.

'I'm not going. I don't feel well.'

'You either go on the stage or you're not in the 4th Year any more.'

Suddenly, the girls around me plead with me to go on stage. They don't want to see me thrown out.

But I am furious with him, so the argument continues.

'There is no way I'm going on stage.'

'Go on stage now, or leave at once.'

I become scared of him, so I make my way to the stage, depleted of energy, but when I try to dance, I put no effort into it. He screams:

'You either do it properly, or... '

I say "fuck off" behind the curtains and leave the stage, as he has become cruel and I can't take it any more.

This memory plays in my mind, just before I enter the Steiner College. Maybe I should have left Eurythmy when I had the chance. May be it took me over the edge.

I see Hikari. She has her black hair in a bun, and is wearing a grey, suede coat.

'Hi, Marcia. You look well,' she says, hugging me.

As I look about me there isn't really anyone I know, so we sit down and wait for the performance to start.

'He is looking at you,' Hikari suddenly says.

I blush and look behind me. He really is. He is smiling broadly and he looks handsome.

I am surprised that he is being so kind, but that same light that shimmers warns me. I have already burnt my bridges with him and won't be going back into the stage group; it is over. Hikari tells me to go and talk to him during the break, but I am too embarrassed by my diagnosis, and the strange letters I had sent him. Before I know it, he has moved to the front of the stage and my chance has gone. I carry on watching the performance, with my heart sinking with every beat of music. Now I am well, I realise how much I took Eurythmy for granted. What in my life can ever replace it?

After the performance, Hikari and I walk into the chilly February night and she says that maybe I can come back into the stage group? She will ask for me. But I know they will not have me back as I never fitted into the group very well.

Eurythmy haunts my mind. I particularly miss my wonderful French teacher who died of a brain tumour, before I got ill. She was the best Eurythmist I'd ever seen, and I was close to her. I remember the last time I saw her – it was the day before she died. I see her as my Spirit Guide now, and I will remember her forever.

When I get home, I cuddle up to my duvet and I decide to do one thing – to pray.

I pray to the Angels, to God and to my Higher self:
Please help me find a new direction in my life.
My illness is a healthy response to an insane world, according to R.D. Laing.

I can't take the news coverage of acts of violence by those with the same illness. So I avoid the papers. 87% of those with my illness are unemployed. That is a little sad. There are rehabilitation programs for prisoners, but I don't know of any for the mentally ill.

It's the spring of 2005 and I've made a decision. I will try to be positive and I will try to get a job. Let me tell you a little about my family though. My dad is a property developer and splits his time between running a shop in Dormansland and running a property business in Montenegro. My older brother works at the Custom's office and my other brother works at a printer's in Hammersmith.

My brother jokes that I have an incurable illness. He also says that the singer of the *Beach Boys* also lost the plot like me.

On this fresh, sunny, spring day, I meet my dad in *The Cage Pub*, in Lingfield.

'How are you, Marcia?'

'I'm okay. I'm on a 15 mg tablet, and I sleep a lot.'

'I'm sure that the doctor will bring you down in time.' He says, kindly.

He has on a black leather jacket and tight jeans. His hair is static and a mess. His deep wrinkles show years of worry, but he is still handsome, in a rugged sort of way.

'I want to go back to Eurythmy!'

'Do you want me to phone them? I can do, if you want me to.'

'Not yet - I'll think about it. I might try and get a new job.'

'Yes, that would be great. What sort of job?'

'As a Teaching Assistant. I have experience as a teacher.'

'I'm sure you will be good at that. You should come and stay with me in Montenegro.'

That night, I settle into my double bed in Dormansland. The beige wall, low ceiling, old pine wardrobe and dirty window haunt me. This is where I became ill.

It's an early shift at 8 a.m. in the shop, then I will take my auntie and grandma back to Crawley.

I have only one friend in Hikari, but the friendship doesn't seem the same since I got ill. Is she judgemental of me? I'm just not sure. I wonder if I will ever have friends again. I am again reminded of the stigma of mental illness. It is not something that is openly discussed in polite society and that's a great shame. My illness has taught me not to judge and to be compassionate towards the mentally ill - and even to myself.

The next day, I have an appointment with the psychiatrist. He is leaving and another one is present, ready to take over his practice.

'This is Marcia. She had a nervous breakdown. She threw away lots of things and heard voices.'

I get a sharp pain in my heart. I have a vague memory of throwing away precious things. I threw them into the dump, never to be retrieved; beautiful photos and medals.

'I have decided to take you down to 12.5 mg.'

'I have put on a lot of weight!'

'You will see a difference in your weight, when we lower the dose.'

I don't want to be here. I don't want to wake up in the morning and find the highlight of my day is to visit a psychiatrist!

I go home and look through the job section of the *Crawley Observer*. I'm 27 with little work experience, as I've spent 4 years training to be an Eurythmist. I decide to apply to be an admin assistant. I like the neat arrangement of the ad in the paper; this gives me hope.

Evening falls - it's 9 p.m. and I decide to go to bed early.

I look outside at the blooming daffodils and the sweet dahlias. The garden is overgrown, and my mum is considering moving, as she can't keep up with it. Since her split from dad she has wanted a home of her own.

The phone rings and mum answers – Hikari is calling. I'm quite surprised, as she rarely calls at that time of night. The line crackles and I can barely hear her.

'Hi, Marcia. How are you? I asked the stage group about the possibility of you coming back, but they said that they are happy with the way the group is at the moment. They don't want any more changes.'

My heart drops. I knew that this would be the outcome, but it hurts anyway.

'Thanks for asking them. Good night.'

I put the phone down, as I don't want to talk to her. Another dream is shattered. It's obvious that they are scared of my diagnosis and are not willing to give me another chance.

Schizophrenia is a splitting away from reality, as introduced by Eugen Bleuler, the Swiss psychiatrist, in 1911.

The light dances above my head again. *Don't give up. Something else will turn up.*

Tears sting my eyes and I fall to sleep, broken hearted.

Chapter Four

The School

For my 28th birthday I go to *ASK* with my mum and my two brothers.

By now, I have lost a little bit of weight and can fit into my long, black, silk skirt and fitted cardigan.

My brother buys me the new *Coldplay* CD and I'm most grateful. I'm down to a 10 mg tablet now, and as my uncle states: "...you still have your whole life ahead of you".

I have my admin assistant interview next month, and though this is not what I want to do, I feel that it could be a stepping-stone for me. Now that I am well, I am convinced that I can come off this medication eventually and this makes me feel relieved. I don't want this diagnosis for the rest of my life.

In July, I go for my interview in a flat building –it is bright and breezy inside. There are fluorescent lights and a small box-like reception area. It has the 9-5 day job feeling. Even the receptionist has a mechanical politeness about her.

I get called to wait outside the room, and soon I'm face-to-face with the manager. He asks me boring questions like: "How do you see yourself in five years time?" He even asks what Eurythmy is and will I go back to it. It is clear from the interview that I am not suitable for the job, and I have holes in my CV.

I was doing beautiful Eurythmy once and now I am applying for an office job.

A couple of weeks later, I get a standard rejection letter: someone else had more suitable experience.

However, something nice happens in July. I bump into Rebecca in East Grinstead in a charity shop. I find out that she is getting married next year. We know each other from Eurythmy days, and we spend the afternoon talking about old times. I had been 21 years old when I enrolled in the Course and Rebecca was in the Year above me. People thought it was hilarious that we were both from Crawley.

'I don't miss Peredur Eurythmy, Marcia.'

'There was so much judgement and those awful, old-fashioned dresses!'

'What actually happened to you, Marcie?'

'Well, I was in the stage group but I never fitted in there.'

'Who could ever fit into Anthroposophy?'

It is so nice to see Rebecca. We have a genuine friendship and she knows about my diagnosis and is accepting of it. As I drive my little red *Nissan* back to my dad's place, I am so happy that I have a friend in this world. I don't need to hide from her, as she understands.

This is a really strange time for me. There are two things I'd love to do: study Reflexology and pursue a musical career.

I've started reading about Reflexology. I love the way that the feet are massaged to treat the whole body – this stimulates the body's own healing process. I am fascinated as to how a Reflexologist can detect imbalances in the body and I remember, in the past, when I had received it, how much I liked it! 7000 nerves in the feet are stimulated by the treatment.

But, blindly, I look for another job and see a vacancy for a Teaching Assistant at a Secondary school. Before too long, I have an interview and get the job!

I am to start in September with another girl, Bella. I have a premonition about this job, as I was worried that I had to lie to get it. On the application form it asked if I had ever had a serious illness, and I ticked the "No" box. I had a feeling that if I was open about it, I just wouldn't get it.

There is something else troubling me. The lady in charge looks like a right cow! From the moment I saw her, I didn't like her. But this still might be my chance for happiness.

The first day, I nervously introduce myself to the school office, and walk up a huge flight of stairs, before entering a spacious room, where teachers are sitting in groups and windows are open. There is a kitchen adjacent to it where people can make cups of tea. As I sit down on a large brown sofa, I have a thought: *"Bono, I wish you'd answered my letters, then I wouldn't be here!"*

I sit down next to a girl who is Polish, but speaks English very well. The first thing that I notice is that the other Teaching Assistants do not acknowledge us.

My first day is spent with Zoë, as she helps children with Special Needs. Zoë warns me that the one in charge is a "bitch". I try to laugh this away, as this is the first proper full time job I've had, but the thought really disturbs me.

Firstly, I find getting up in the morning to be there for 9 a.m. very hard, as I'm groggy in the morning from the medication. Secondly, there is a clerical side to the job that I have no clue about. A fellow teaching assistant tries to explain certain procedures, unsuccessfully, so I only end up stuffing letters and writing addresses. But, as the weeks go on, I love the classroom side of the job, and get to know some of the children. Jemma has special needs and gets behind in most lessons. Sally is sweet and I help her in Science classes. But the cracks start to show.

Early on in the job I have to fill in a medical questionnaire that is supposedly confidential. I have to disclose my illness. It must be even worse if you've been in prison. I find this is unfair, as I've only had a one-off breakdown. When I read what the doctor has written, I think that I'm not going to last in this job very long.

He wrote: *"Marcia has been diagnosed with paranoid Schizophrenia and has had a psychotic breakdown".*

The woman in charge also starts to become difficult.

At 9 a.m. in the morning all of the Teaching Assistants are upstairs talking, until lessons start at 9.20 a.m. Yet the Senco rings from her office and says I must go to her immediately.

'Your job starts at 9 a.m. not 9.20 a.m.!'

'But the other Teaching Assistants are there too!' I reply.

'That's up to me to sort out, not you! Right... I want you to do this for me.'

Every morning she gives me tasks to do, while the other Teaching Assistants do nothing. I have to disturb a teacher in a classroom, photocopy things, and input data. There is something else, which is unfair. Some Periods are for office work, so I would go to her office and she wouldn't be there. So, I would go back to the Staff Room and read.

As the months go on, I realise that I am being bullied. Although I am still healthy on medication, I have no assertive skills and I start to hate myself for not biting back at her. Every single day I dread doing the job, because of her. There is also an incident when she shouted at me, in front of the other Teaching Assistants and showed me up. Every day, when I go home, I am so relieved that I don't have to see her until the next day. What I'm experiencing is pure and utter discrimination. No wonder 87% of people with my diagnosis are unemployed!

All I can do is try and keep it together. I don't want to disappoint my mum, as it's the first time I've had my own income. But things just get worse and worse. I start to hate the job. None of the children like the Senco, as a lot of them get shouted at by her. And, it all comes down to one final day. I'm in the classroom, while the Senco is observing me on my Appraisal. Afterwards, I go to her office and she says:

'You've done very well in your Appraisal. You are good with the children. But I'm not happy with other aspects of your job.'

I knew it... here comes the avalanche.

'You do not get on well with the other Teaching Assistants - Joanne does all of the office work and she is overwhelmed.'

'I did not want to do the clerical work!' I blurt out.

'That was advertised as part of the job! Plus, you do not listen to instructions and... you've managed to lose Joanne's key.'

'That was only once.' I bite back. 'I really need to have a think about this.'

'Whether this is the job for you?' She asks.

Again, tears sting my eyes. I feel like a failure. I can't even hold down a T.A. job! The next day, I am in a pensive mood. The truth is, although I don't gel with the other T.A.'s, I do have my own group of friends. Bella is also on the outside, but she puts that down to her lack of English – but she speaks it perfectly well!

Another T.A. hands me a letter in the staff room – it's a list of everything that I must improve in the job. I decide there and then that I'm going to hand in my Notice. I am badly disappointed, but can't take the stress anymore. It is clear to me that I am being discriminated against. Unfortunately, it is the Law that people with mental illness must disclose their illness.

The next day, I tell her that I've decided to hand in my Notice and she accepts it easily. This was her plan - to push me out - and she has achieved it.

Just a week later, I am moving house with mum. We are going to live in a smaller house in Tilgate. This is good, because it takes my mind off what has happened but I feel so sad to leave Theydon Close.

In my new bedroom, there are boxes full of photos, memorabilia, books and CDs – but no furniture as yet. And something else is wrong. I went to my last meeting with the doctor. He said that I could come off my medication in two months time, but I have come off it now.

I am in the world of U2 again. I am looking for a form of escape, as I am so unhappy about the job experience. Slowly, I start to lose grip on reality again. At first, my mum puts up with me; she makes me soup and bread, as I forget to eat. All day long, I am hearing voices again. It is like there is a physiological change in my body.

I want to make it clear for those who don't understand about mental illness, that I have no control over the voices as they take over me. These voices are full of hope for my new life. They have tricks, and different shades and they know me better than anyone.

My dad starts to stay with my mum, who is stressed with me.

I spend £100's on make-up and clothes and I let my dad see me naked. Before I know it, there is a police car pulling up inside our driveway and I realise that it is happening again. So, I lock myself in the bathroom. A lot of male policemen are in the house, trying to communicate with me. I give in and go to lie on my bed.

'Come on Marcia, come down with us.'

They are almost flirting with me. Some of them are enjoying having this control over me.

'You're a fucking bastard. And you're a fucking bastard!'

'Come on Marcia, you need to come with us.'

'Can I go to prison instead?'

'Yes okay.' They almost laugh.

It is supposed to be tragic, but it's all rather funny. I think that I am going to prison! I get handcuffed and sit on the back seat with a nice policeman. He has a kind face. But, it's happening again. I'm being sectioned.

Chapter Five

The Apple Tree

When I was a little girl, we had an apple tree in our back garden. I used to marvel at these apples and take one to school every day. I wore a denim dress and I had beautiful dreams for the future. I used to sing Abba's *I Have A Dream*. When you're little, you never believe anything bad is ever going to happen to you. You believe in Angels and fairies. What was so special about this apple tree? It talked to me without words.

You never know what is going to happen to you when you grow up. I know that I never wanted to grow up – and maybe that's part of my illness... I still have a childlike naivety. I see the world through rose-tinted glasses.

Rebecca says: "It's hard to be on this earth when you're so innocent". But am I innocent?

The apple tree holds beautiful memories for me. I was really going to do something special in the future. I was going to help people.

Who knows what has happened to that apple tree? Is it still alive? It is certainly still alive in my heart and big, juicy apples come not from the supermarket - but from that tree!

Chapter Six

Rose Ward Again

I'm sitting in the car with a nice policeman. I know he is kind, because he is talking to me about music and he has a gentle manner. He has brown, flicked back hair, brown eyes and he wears a sturdy uniform.

'So... what sort of music do you like?' He says.

'I like lots of different types.' I reply.

'Do you like *The Killers* and *U2*? How old are you? You look 26-27.'

'I like *The Killers* but Bono's a fucking bastard!'

'Do you like British bands?'

'Yes, I like *Blur* and *Oasis*.' I reply.

'What singer/songwriters do you like?' He says.

'I like Joni Mitchell. Can I have some water?'

'Very soon.'

'I also like Kate Bush.' I say.

'She hasn't done much lately.'

'She's scared to perform, like me.'

'Have you performed much?'

'A little bit.'

And so the conversation goes on.

I'm forgetting that I'm even supposed to be ill.

Strangely, I think of Christina Rosetti's poem:

Perhaps some day, who knows?
But not today; it froze, and blows and snows,
And you're too curious: fie!
You want to hear it? well:
Only, my secret's mine, and I won't tell.

Winter My Secret by Christina Georgina Rossetti.

Rosetti was around in the Victorian period. She always defended the weak and vulnerable. Her poems often have double meanings, and a lively, teasing voice. She wrote during the Industrial age, and her poems convey a spiritual world, reflecting a material one. Her speaking voice in her poems often has a mask or a persona.

This is why I'm thinking of her. I'm being stripped of my persona. Not a single person is able to talk to me when I'm ill, but this policeman is able to do so. He is talking to me like I'm not ill. The policeman is not afraid. I don't believe he is just doing a job; he actually cares.

It's like I've had a secret all my life, and the policeman gets it. It is beautiful.

I arrive at Rose Ward, disappointed that it's not a prison. The lifeless building glares at me and my throat tightens. As I climb the stairs, the policeman calls out: "...see you when you're famous". My heart lightens and he is gone.

I am led into a familiar looking room. There is a doctor and nurse there. The doctor wants to do a quick check-up, and I ask the nurse for some water. For some reason, she looks nervous, and shows heartfelt sympathy for me. It's probably because she remembers me from the last time I was there. I have it in my mind that I need Morrissey's address, and I ask the doctor if he can get it for me.

He looks bewildered:

'I don't have Morrissey's address!'

There is only one thing that I feel like doing when I'm there and that is sleeping.

I want to explain to you what hearing voices feels like.

They can take you over, and it's not just a mental change – it's physical too.

My throat tightens, and sometimes I can hardly breathe. The voices aren't the hard thing to deal with – they never want to do harm to other people.

It is a myth that people with Schizophrenia are violent. I enjoy my voices. They are like my friends. But no matter how much I hope they will get me out of a sticky situation, they never actually do.

During the night, the nurse pops in to see how I am; looking genuinely concerned. She is probably a similar age to me and is an African-American. Her hair is pulled back in a tight bun – her eyes are expressive and she is pretty. She seems to connect with me on a soul level. As I wake up the next morning, my voices are not helpful at all. Bono is banging on my door again. This time I am prepared, so I've managed to bring a pen and paper. I guess it's time for the job in hand. I will write another letter to Bono. I don't want to think whether he will reply or not. I convince myself that he will. I write a short letter - similar to the one I wrote before. But just before I do, I have a flashback of the doctor who came in the middle of the night to my room and put a spotlight on me. It was flirtatious. The strange thing is, I have a John Lennon tape in my knickers, and by the time the morning comes, it is gone. This really troubles me. I don't like it at all.

I know this time is going to be hard. I walk down the corridor and lose the plot and scream: "My family is evil". I don't really believe this, but I can't understand what I'm doing back inside a psychiatric ward.

Two nurses come to my room and say:

"You either take this tablet or we will forcibly inject you".

I think this is not right. They could've just asked me to take the tablet, and I would have anyway. It is lonely inside a psychiatric ward. The feeling of being locked in causes so much anxiety to a patient. I think I write letters and poems to keep myself entertained. In the evening, I walk to have my dinner.

It is like being at school again. I notice another girl laughing at me because I smell. She is cruel and she is probably not well either. She probably doesn't want to be here either. She has brown eyes and long, blonde hair that is tied back in a ponytail. This time I notice quite a lot of girls on the ward. There is another girl called Claire who self-harms; her arms have cuts on them. The meal is cauliflower cheese, which is disgusting, but I have to eat it, as I'm starving hungry. But something nice happens to me here. I make friends with a boy called Stephen. It isn't romantic or anything like that, but it helps to stabilize me. We watch DVDs and he says that I'm pretty. He tries to explain to me that being here is nowhere near the same as being in prison. There is another guy hanging around called Sean. He is good looking, with a sturdy frame and deep blue eyes. For the first time ever, I start to like being inside a psychiatric ward. There are Art Classes in the day, relaxation classes in the evening, and also my letter writing to Bono.

Stephen said: 'Shall we watch a DVD together?'

'Okay, but as long as it's not scary. '

So we watch it and he says: 'That girl in it, looks like you.'

'No it doesn't. She's prettier than me.'

'You would look the same with make-up on!'

It does occur to me that Stephen may have a crush on me, but I only want to be friends. I realise that part of my problem is I just don't have friends. I live with my mum in the shadow of a job that went badly wrong and I wish that things were different.

One great distraction in the ward is the pool table. I am excellent at beating any opponent that comes my way, including Stephen.

At night I watch *EastEnders*, and my mum visits most days. I like the independence that I have from her, and I realise how much I need my own space now.

A couple of weeks fly by and I am nearly completely better. While I'm in the dormitory, Stephen calls out: 'Where is the pretty girl?'

When I get leave, I go round Horsham town with my mum, but I feel spaced out, as I'm not used to being outside in the world. Lucky for me, I don't get institutionalised, like some of the other patients.

Something special happens on my 29th birthday.

I celebrate with my family at my brother's house in Northgate, dreaming of Bono. I start to wish for a better future and a brand new start. My brother makes an observation that surprises me. He says: 'It's better than working in a full time job".

I'm not so sure about this. I feel all of my life that I'm hanging on to hope, and my big hope now is that Bono will reply. Only a mentally ill person could possibly even conceive of this.

When I go back to the ward, there is one really pleasant Sunday where my dad and brothers visit me and we play pool. It's harder to beat them, and it reminds me of holidays in the past, when we've had such fun together. When you are locked up inside, you really start to take pleasure in the little things in life.

Eventually, I am well enough to go home, and I meet my new CPN, Mike, at the Weald Day Centre at Crawley hospital. He tells me that the media image of people with Schizophrenia doesn't portray the reality: it shows them as being violent, when they are usually placid.

He also explains that there are two types of Schizophrenia: paranoid - which is treatable - and normal Schizophrenia, which is much harder to treat. 40% of people tend to suffer from the paranoid type. I find Mike very helpful, and he also introduces me to Southdown Housing, which provides support and housing services to vulnerable people throughout

Sussex. They work to increase independence and to help everyone, regardless of their disability.

They support 7,150 people in the Sussex area, providing housing support and employment, care and community services.

I find the idea of having my own place very exciting.

Part of the reason I'm writing this book is to break down the stigma that exists, and to get this illness in the spotlight, where people can really see it.

It is sad that we are made to be silent, increasing loneliness and even madness.

There has to be another way.

I believe that a negative self-image is often compensated by an overblown, archetypal one. It's a shame that more doctors do not understand this.

There are a couple of things that dwell on my mind at the age of 29.

I want to do a course in something and I want to make new friends.

One afternoon, while I'm having coffee with my mum, I decide to send off the deposit to *The Central College of Reflexology*. I want to do something that keeps me active and that gives me some career prospects. Then... there is Rafe. I met him on the Internet, and we went out a few times in London. I was afraid of telling him about my diagnosis and I wasn't sure that I fancied him. After a while, he stopped contacting me and I have not seen him since.

The diagnosis of Schizophrenia can greatly affect your life. It's something you have to hide, for fear of people's responses.

I only hope that one day my diagnosis will be out in the open, and I will find a man who is accepting of it. But, for now, I only have one goal in mind - to start my Reflexology course.

Chapter Seven

Regret

I'm very excited to start my Reflexology course; I guess it gives me something to focus on.

It's also around this time that I go to lunch with my dad and he hands me £500 for the course. That will pay for half of it. It still amazes me how generous my dad can be.

The Central London College of Reflexology has been going since 1989 and has a solid international base. It is in the heart of Covent Garden, quite near to the Underground. It will give me an *ABC Level 3 Diploma in Reflexology*, which is the highest award you can have.

I vividly remember my first day there. I had a rush of anxiety as I got the train to Victoria, and had even more worry as I boarded the Tube and changed at Green Park Station. As I walked from the Tube to the College, the sun glared in my eyes, and there was frost hanging in the air, even though it was October.

I buzzed the entry button, and stated that I was a student, and I walked up the concrete stairs to where I was supposed to be. As I entered, Mike took my jacket, and there is a small reception area, and three rooms in a semi-circle around it. The room I entered had a glass door, and there are hand and foot Reflexology charts on the wall.

It was a small, cosy room where a couple of students were sitting.

We had to fill in a medical questionnaire. *"Oh no, not this again,"* I think.

I don't want to write about my diagnosis, so I instead write that I take *Olanzapine*, for depression. It isn't for depression, but I don't want to admit the truth.

The students start gathering and I get talking to a Brazilian guy, who seems friendly enough. Then we play a couple of games, that are meant to help us get to know one another, and we learn a little about Anatomy and Physiology. In the afternoon we start to learn some of the sequence. It is a long day and I had to come back the next day too; the course is organised over the weekend, to suit people who work during the week.

When I go home, I have a thumping headache and painkillers don't make any difference.

The good thing is, for the first couple of months, I make friends with a Brazilian guy and a Greek guy. We eat together in a nearby café. I don't know if we will stay in touch after the course, but, for now, it is nice to socialise. This course gives my life structure. I start to plan my days and weeks, and I begin to work on my case studies.

Around this time, I see a man at Workability, about trying to get back into the work place. It is the second time that I've been on this scheme, but very little help is offered.

One day, someone must come up with a strategy or a solution to help the mentally ill back to work. Employers must be educated not to discriminate potential employees who have a mental illness.

My support worker at Workability made me aware of how the stigma exists in our language – they say someone is *mad* or *crazy*. We use this language every day and we need to be more aware of its widespread connotations.

I lost a lot of confidence during my time at the School and I am scared about being bullied again, because of my diagnosis.

My dad said that he had phoned the headmaster of the school, who had apologised about my illness being disclosed.

There is something else that changes me for the better in the autumn of 2006.

I go and see a therapist called Sara. My mother had been seeing her for Kinesiology. She had mentioned my diagnosis and she thought that she could help me.

It is easy for me to dip down into depression; I don't really suffer from depression, but I lost a lot of confidence after having two breakdowns.

When I visit Sara she is just what I need. She has white, porcelain teeth, a beautiful smile and a cheerful disposition. She reminds me of the existence of Angels, and tells me to read a book by Brandon Bays called *The Journey*.

That November, my mum and I take a trip to Cyprus and stay at a 5-star hotel. Unfortunately, it isn't warm, and the inside pool is closed, so the only thing we look forward to is the delicious food at 7 p.m. The holiday is a wash out, but I do a lot of reading, especially the Brandon Bays book.

So... what is *The Journey* all about? The author, Brandon Bays, had a tumour the size of a basketball and managed to heal herself without chemo. In doing so, she initiated the healing work that became *The Journey*. *The Journey* is where old, emotional patterns that have been stored in cells, can be healed by the process of hypnotherapy - with the help of a trained practitioner.

The whole time that I was in Cyprus, I was looking forward to seeing Sara again. A holiday rejuvenates your mind.

A few days later, I see Sara, in her lovely room that is full of crystals and incense.

'Hi, Marcia, how are you?'

'I'm fine, thanks.' Sara's teeth were gleaming again.

'Did you read the book?'

'Yes, I thought that it was great!'

'One thing that I think you should do, is get rid of that label: Schizophrenia. Write the word down on a piece of paper and burn it!'

'That sounds like a good idea – and, I also have a problem about taking medication.'

'Then, I have a new Affirmation for you: *I let go of my fear of Medication.* You don't have to feel ashamed of taking medication.'

Seeing Sara was quite expensive. I had four healing and therapeutic sessions with her that cost £90 each. She took me back to key moments in my life where I suffered trauma and I would have to picture light and a healing resolution to this trauma.

I'm not sure that all we went over worked. I do believe in Angels and the afterlife, but I also believe in free will - and that we are solely responsible for our own lives. It was great to come to terms with my fear of medication, but, whether I liked it or not, I had been diagnosed with Schizophrenia. In the end, I stopped going to see Sara – but felt that I had benefited from a lot that we talked about.

In 2007, the spring had an expansive quality. Daffodils sprung up in the garden, and the big fish swam happily in my mum's pond. It seems like we can wait for spring forever but this spring I enjoyed travelling to my Course in London and socialising with people.

Every Monday afternoon, I go to the cinema on my own and enjoy a selection of films. Then, afterwards, I meet my mum for a coffee. She works in a Family Planning Clinic. We always discuss endless topics but, most of all; we love to talk about how doctors are narrow-minded.

'Mum, there must be a way to treat people with mental illness, without the use of drugs.'

'Mental illness is another dimension, Marcia.'

And so the conversation would go on.

Recently, Dr. B. reduced my medication and I started to lose weight again. He is kind but isn't very open to me coming off it all together. I am quickly signed off by the Mental Health Services, because I am doing so well.

You forget what it feels like to be ill, and it's quite a temptation to come off medication altogether.

In the summer of 2007, I celebrate my 30th birthday. My family and I go to a posh restaurant in Brighton. I have fish soup, which is so delicious that my taste buds are on fire! I feel so guilty about how I treated my family when I was ill. I guess that I couldn't help it.

I should explain about my parents. They are separated, but are still friends and we meet as a family amicably. My dad bought a shop in Dormansland and started his own property developing business. Both my parents are like rocks to me. In a way, they over protect me, but this is better than being negligent.

On my 30th birthday celebration, there is laughter and pleasant conversation. I believe they want to make it nice for me, because of what I had been through. I'm lucky to have a close-knit family. I believe that if I didn't, I could have ended up on the streets.

Just after my birthday, I spend a week at my aunties. I do a couple of Reflexology treatments on her and she takes some photos of me. I notice that I have aged slightly and don't have the plump face that I had in my 20's.

Around this time, mum and I visit an acupuncturist – a frail lady called Jane, but when her clinic prices go up, we stop going. Then she phoned my mum and told her that we could see her at her home - £70 for two people - and this sounds like a good idea to us.

We travel by car, through the winding roads and the piercing rain, and my mother nearly gets lost.

Eventually, we find the smart, detached house. It is very clean cut and big inside, with an old pine piano.

Sometimes you feel trouble tripping you up or tingling down your spine.

My one weakness is that I tend to believe what anyone tells me. I'm too naïve. As I walk into the small therapy room, I know what is coming.

'Are you taking medication?'

'Yes, I am.

'You need to come off it. It's harming you.'

'My mother doesn't want me to.'

'I will talk to her.'

My mother is called into the room. There is a very worried look on her face.

'She needs to come off her medication.'

'She's been sectioned. I don't want to go through it all again.'

'If it happens, it happens. She should try to come off this medication.'

As much as I like Complementary therapists, some can't be trusted. Because I had worked with Sara and had been having acupuncture with Jane, I thought that I might be able to come off it. There was no major stress in my life. What if the medication really was doing me long term damage? In a way, Jane and I bullied my mother into agreeing to me coming off it. All I took was a 5 mg tablet; would it really make such a difference?

I go home and decide that night not to take my tablet. The first thing that happens is I can't sleep. Then, the next day, I feel completely spaced out. Where is the support for those with mental illness in moving away from long-term medication?

That night I dream of Bono again.

He is seeping back into my dreams. I can hear his voice telling me to write him letters. There is a tiny part of my being that is aware that it's happening all again.

I'm becoming unwell for the third time, and I feel sad for my mother.

Chapter Eight

The Last Time In Rose Ward

I remember a picture that will stay with me forever.

I'm listening to U2 in my bedroom, and I come downstairs into the conservatory; a brightly lit room with a pink sofa and a tiled floor. My electric piano is on the other side. My mum is sitting in an *Ikea* chair, crying. I know that I am responsible for this.

Despite all that is written about people with Schizophrenia being *unfeeling*, I feel empathy for my mum. Somewhere inside of me, I know that I should have stayed on my medication. This is just so stressful for her.

The doorbell rings and it's the psychiatrist. I quickly walk outside the garden to get away. I go over the little, wooden bridge, and stare at the fish in the pond. The psychiatrist dives me a playful wink and has a kind look on his face.

Throughout the previous days, I've been writing to U2, eating veggie burgers, smoking *Mayfair Lights*, and singing my songs on the piano.

My mother gives me soup and bread, and again I feel that the *Vittel* water is poisonous and I must drink *Evian* instead.

My dad comes round – and my parents lock the door.

I scream at my mum to unlock it.

I need to post a letter. I want to make that clear. There are some things I do have control over and some things that I don't. I really believe these trickster voices when they tell me to post letters to various people.

The doctor asks to talk to me and I agree.

'Do you have any friends?'

I find this a peculiar question, so I reply: 'I have friends in the Netherlands.'

The truth is, I have one friend in the Netherlands, whom I never see, and we just send Xmas cards to each other.

'How is it with your family?'

'I feel that I am more educated and cultured than them.'

'Would you like to come to hospital?'

'Okay.'

This is a strange reply, but I'm fed up with being sectioned, and at least I will have the honour of going to hospital voluntarily. They can't force you to take medication that way.

My dad drives me to Rose Ward in his green BMW, and Morrissey is playing in the background. I've brought a few things with me: a note pad, some pictures, a toothbrush and a picture of an Angel, torn from an old calendar.

There is no conversation in the car, as I'm feeling really down. Why do I keep being admitted to hospital?

When we arrive, I blank my father as he tells my name to the receptionist and, when I'm inside, I keep asking him to go away. He finally gives in and leaves. This time, I am in the dormitory at the end, next to the window.

That night, they ask if I want medication and I say no.

I hardly sleep at all. There is a new preoccupation that I have. I can't decide what I want to do with my life, so I decide that I am meant to do everything. I'm an Eurythmist, also an actress, a poet, a singer, an athlete, etc.

I start to write silly letters to Gordon Brown about how I've suffered an injustice and tell him that I am in a psychiatric ward but, I'm really meant to be treading the boards in the West End. I'm having delusions of grandeur again.

Around this time, in a delusional state, I send a text to my friend Hikari, telling her that she is not a good Eurythmist. She sends one back, asking how I dare to say that to her. She doesn't realise I'm unwell and I've just lost the only true friend I have.

Mental illness can isolate you and ruin parts of your life.

As I walk around Rose Ward at 11 a.m. on a cold day, I start to feel claustrophobic. I know that the door is locked, so I ask to go into the garden, but the nurse says:

"You can't go out, until you take your medication!"

Now I'm stuck. I have voices in my head, I'm exhausted and I'm lonely.

I decide that I will just have to take the medication; otherwise I will not be let outside.

My mother visits and we go into a small room without windows. I put on U2's, *A Beautiful Day*. She has a toy monkey with her, and does a funny voice, whilst wriggling him around. I'm not in the mood for ventriloquism, so I throw the monkey across the room.

'Can you post a letter for me?'

My mother is not enthusiastic about it. I know in my heart that the letter will not get an answer, but these letters help me to focus on something – they also help me to cope with my illness.

'Will you come again tomorrow?'

'I'm working tomorrow. I'll come on Wednesday.'

Even in my madness, I am lonely and appreciate my mother's visit.

In the evening, I am given *Rispiridone* – a different drug, that doesn't make me put on weight.

I have my first night's sleep in a long time, but the drug is not as effective as *Olanzapine*. I'm obsessed with not putting on weight, so I endure the side effects: restlessness and anxiety.

The day after I take it, I faint and two nurses have to accompany me to my bed. I see a piercing light, which nearly blinds me, then I look at an Angel poster on the wall and the light is gone. It actually felt like I was going to die, but it was probably the side effects from the drug.

Last time I wrote poetry inside, but this time I play a keyboard and go to Art Classes. I tend to play my own songs that I compose on the piano. In the Art Class, I meet a lovely lady called Jan who has short, blonde hair, a slender frame and a very pleasant manner. I simply colour in some flowers and draw some of my own too. The therapeutic effects of Art are well known. It enables us to be released from trauma, and is a powerful form of expression. It also helps by getting us in touch with our feelings, and our spiritual side. I know that it is aiding my recovery.

Later on in the day, I take part in a cookery class with only one other person; a jittery boy - so I have to do all of it by myself. I cut up vegetables, and then we roast them in the oven. It is a pleasure to eat them, and they taste very crispy.

All in all, my third time in Rose Ward is not a bad experience. There is one young girl who I have an argument with, after I play *Imagine* too loud, and disturb everyone. She threatens to kill me, and then, a day later, we play pool together, as if nothing has happened. She is small, with a pretty, delicate featured face. There is also another nice woman in there, who is Indian, and has a little girl who comes to visit her. I give her some nice prayers from one of my books and we eat Indian takeaway together. She is plump, with a high voice, and beautiful long, black hair.

The problem with making friends in a psychiatric ward, is you never know if you will still be friends when you get out of there. I think that I liked being in there, because I enjoyed having friends.

Pretty soon, I am given leave, and mum and I walk around Horsham town centre. It is nice just to get some fresh air. I was bored with walking up and down the walled garden. That same day, there is a meeting to discuss if I could go home. My parents, two psychiatrists and a social worker are present. My mum says: "...she still wants to be called Maria". At this, I become angry, as it is up to me what I want to be called. My voices still call me Maria.

'Why not be called Marcia and what about Reflexology?'

No one can understand me at this point, so my dad takes my hand and says to them all: "She will be fine. Everything will be okay".

I walk out of the meeting upset. I don't like my own name any more. That day, I go back home and we have a family meal, but I do not say a word. The truth is, that I do not feel as well on this drug as on *Olanzapine*. I do not sleep as well either. I tell my psychiatric nurse that I need to change my medication and, after I pick up the new medication, I have a dream. In the dream I am told that I should carry on with my Reflexology Course and not be so judgemental about the new psychiatrist. There is an angelic feeling to the dream and it spurs me to take action.

I think one of the most important things to do, when recovering from a mental illness is to stay busy and keep focused. After that dream, I make a promise to myself to try to stay positive and do something with my life. The dream gives me the lift I need.

Not long after I am discharged, my auntie has her 60th birthday party in a busy hall, with bright swirling lights. I do my best to enjoy the occasion, but I really

53

miss the friends I made at Rose Ward.

I spend too many days alone and that is not really good for me, but enrolling in a gym gives me some new focus. I also have Art Therapy sessions on a Monday afternoon, and I talk a lot to my therapist about how I dislike my diagnosis.

She is very caring and understanding and helps me to come to terms with it.

We spend Xmas at my brother's house in Northgate, playing games and watching TV and, in January, I go back to the Reflexology Course and meet up with my Brazilian and Greek friends.

Just by chance, the subject of mental illness comes up in one of our classes, and a boy in the class tells us that his sister has paranoid Schizophrenia. He says that the whole time she was ill, there was another part of her that knew she was ill, but couldn't stop it.

That's exactly how it feels. You want to stop what's happening to your mind but you just can't.

During this time, my Nan was in a Home and my mum and I visited her once or twice a week. She has dementia. I feel a connection with her, as I can see how she has become reliant on being at the Home. If the medication hadn't worked, that could have happened to me. I know that dementia is a different illness, but they both affect the brain. My grandmother is a sweet soul and probably does not remember my mum and I visiting her.

There are so many people struggling in life: the elderly, the mentally ill and the homeless, and yet there is a light within all of us.

Light is grace and grace happens to us all at some stage in our lives.

Chapter Nine

Paris

Soon the spring has come, and the birds are singing in the early morning.

I'm preparing for my Reflexology exam in May, and looking forward to a trip to Paris with my mum.

I also decide that I am never going back into a psychiatric ward again. It just wastes too much time - I want to enjoy my life and live in the present.

One sunny, spring day, I get a phone call from Wendy who works at the Southdown Housing Association. She tells me that there is a lovely, spacious flat available in Broadfield. I visit the flat with my mum, and we discover it is just down the road from my auntie. As I step inside, I notice the bottle green carpet, and the dull beige walls. There is a bathroom to the left and a bedroom to the right. The living room is straight ahead, and quite roomy, but the kitchen needs most work, as there are strange purple flowers on the walls.

It is a very exciting time for me, as I have never had my own place, and really need my independence at the age of 30. I instantly take a liking to the flat and agree to move into it in May. My dad agrees to pay for everything, and my mum knows someone who can decorate it. Before I know it, the walls are painted, the shower fixed, and the kitchen lights and curtain rails are put up.

It is ironic that I only got the flat because I have a disability.

Sometimes, good things can come from unpleasant experiences.

One of the first things I notice when I look around, is the cat flap. I need to get a cat! I think I will wait a little while and then get one. I now have a small car and a flat. All of my life I've been with my mum and we both need our freedom!

The exam comes around quickly, and I have to get a train to Victoria and then the Tube to Leicester Square. I get a little lost, but eventually find the Actor's Community Hall. I am nervous as I sit down. But when I start the exam, the questions are not too hard, and I know the whole History of Reflexology section.

I go home excited. I think that I've passed and have the feeling that Paris is calling.

A day later, mum and I take the *Eurostar* to the centre of Paris, and then a taxi to the small hotel - the holiday was on offer from the *Daily Mail.*

All I want to do in Paris is visit the Eiffel Tower, and the Sacre Coer. But, on the first day, we go to an art gallery that has many exquisite paintings by Picasso, Chagall and Monet. It is so expensive to eat and drink in Paris: an orange juice and a *Coke* is £7!

On the second day we visit the Eiffel Tower. It was built in 1889, and is one of the most wonderful sights in the world. It's the tallest building in Paris, and was built by Gustave Eiffel. There are three levels to it, and there is a great, long queue for the top floor of the tower. As we climb the first level, we have some lunch in the restaurant, and try to get the courage to go to the next level.

We gradually begin our ascent, and suddenly I notice that the railings are all open, and we can see how high up we are. I climb as quickly as I can; my mum huffs and puffs behind me. Soon, we are on the middle level and jubilant to have made it.

There are crowds of people taking photos and I manage to take some too.

While I'm up there, I think about the highs and lows of my life, and I realise this is one of the highs. I know that, even with my diagnosis, I can lead a normal life. I may be on medication, but no one would ever know.

It is a triumphant day and we go back to the hotel exhausted, but elated.

The next day is our last in Paris, and we visit the Sacre Coer. This is a particular favourite of mine, as it is so beautiful inside. It is a Roman Catholic Church, dedicated to the sacred heart of Jesus and is situated at the highest part of the city. It was built in 1875 and finished in 1914. As we enter, I notice the stained glass windows, beautifully lit candles and also a great sense of solitude. There is a large cross with Jesus on it, and I say a prayer for happiness.

We spend almost an hour just sitting in quietude and taking it all in, but we are delighted to go back outside, and witness the hazy sun.

I am looking forward to moving into to my flat, so I decide that weekend to just make the move, and on my first night in my flat I look around pleased with myself. There is a cheap, beige carpet on the floor, as the flat is not permanent, but the new paint on the walls makes such a difference. I still have to wait for my sofa though.

That first night, my brother visits and congratulates me. I feel strange when I'm left alone though, as I'm not used to being on my own. I decide to definitely get a cat.

The following Monday, Mark, my support worker, visits me. He is thin with receding hair and has a kind, gentle manner. He helps me with budgeting and setting up my direct debits.

Southdown Housing is a great service for those who can't manage on their own; I am lucky to have a flat.

I really have a great sense of expectation this summer and it feels like the world is my oyster. I go into my emails and discover that I have passed my Reflexology exam! I have no idea what will come of gaining this qualification, but it is a great sense of achievement anyway.

I can't emphasise enough that I believe people with disabilities should reach for their dreams... no matter what.

So, this is a happy summer for me. But there is one big thing missing in my life, and that is friendship. All of the friends I have made in my life I managed to lose, and this was partly down to my mental illness.

I'd lost Hikari because I sent her a nasty text when I was ill and I really regret it.

I lost my friends from abroad, because I threw all of their letters away, when I was ill. The friends I made in the Ward were only short-term. So, I start to pray for friends. You never know where you might find them again. Then, I thought of Rebecca. She had sent me a card and I tried phoning her, but we just kept missing each other and leaving messages on our phones. She was also settled, with a young family.

One day, out of the blue, I receive a phone call from my brother, who asks if I want an eight-week-old black kitten. I jump at the chance – a little kitten all to myself! I must admit I'm not used to cats, but I so much needed a friend. And, soon after our chat, my brother turned up with the kitten... the cutest thing ever!

Chapter Ten

A Little Dip

The kitten takes a good look around my flat and seems content with what it sees. A black moggy, with an interesting white bow-tie shape around its neck, she was handed over by my brother's work colleague. As she leaves, she says: "Thank you for giving her a home".

But, the truth is, none of us knew the actual sex of the kitten yet!

When I come back to the flat in the evening I feel some trepidation. I didn't realise how scared I was of cats. I try shutting my bedroom door, but the kitten scratches the door and cries. In the end, I give in and start to play with it, by holding a stick with a teddy bear at the end. The kitten is so lively, and climbs up the curtain and leaps from the windowsill.

At 10 p.m. I don't know what to do to get the kitten to sleep, so my mum comes round, and sings lullabies to it; patting its heart. Eventually the kitten gets to sleep.

It is really hard work having a kitten, as they are not allowed outside, until they are neutered. I consider giving the kitten away, but I would feel so guilty if the kitten didn't find a decent home. In the end, I decide to keep it.

Every morning, the kitten cries for food, and I get up at around 6.30 a.m. I then play with it for 30 minutes, then disappear to my mum's house to get some rest. But it is not long until the kitten gets *cat depression,* as it longs to go outside. I eventually give in to the pleading and I remember the first time that the kitten went out. It looked like it was in ecstasy as it gazed up at the sky and felt the gentle breeze. It was fascinated with the birds too; could not take its eyes off of them! I have a yard of my own, and there is a gap in the fence that leads through to the main communal garden. I had to hold on to the kitten's tail to stop it from going any further than my back yard.

Every morning I wake up early and let the kitten out, and then I nap on the sofa with the TV on. Usually *This Morning* is on, and, as I sleep, I can hear the murmuring coming from the TV. Then, suddenly, the kitten comes to me and tells me all about what it got up to outside. Of course, it is speaking in cat language, but I understand it perfectly. It lies on my chest and sleeps with me too. But, at night, it cries for its mother. Can I replace her?

It is not long until the kitten gets neutered.

The vet is a kind man with white hair and looks like Father Christmas. It is amazing to discover that the kitten is in fact a boy! I can't believe it!

My mum then suggests we call the kitten 'Indy' after Indiana Jones. I really like that name. My dad texts me to tell me: "...boy kittens always need more love". All this time, I've been calling him a Princess!

The adventures are to continue with Indy.

His new craze is climbing trees, and it takes him a while to figure out how to get down again. He also loves to catch birds! He brought in a nearly dead pigeon once, and I had to slowly watch it die!

I experience a couple of flashbacks from the second time I'm admitted into hospital: I have my period and

I'm in pain. I ask the nurse if I can go and buy some sanitary towels. She has the utmost compassion for me. *Running To Stand Still* is playing in the background. It's like the story of my life. I appreciate Bono's voice so much. Ouch... my period is hard. Later that day, a nurse comes in and says: "Confetti". I have torn up so many pieces of paper. She also says the letter to Bono has been sent!

Just as this is a difficult time, I also remember a strange incident. The following day, a priest came to visit patients in Rose Ward. I tell him my name is Maria. He says: "Do you know the song *I Have A Dream* by Abba?" I tell him that was my favourite song when I was a little girl. He then says: "In about six months' time you will realise that you met an angel".

I tell him how I believe in angels. I am opening up to a complete stranger, but somehow I know *he* is an angel that has come to visit me. I can't be absolutely sure of this, but I think so. All of my life I've had experiences like that.

Once, in my early twenties, my car broke down and a mechanic turned up in the middle of the night. I think that I am really blessed.

Back to where I am now.

Although I love having a kitten, it is stressful. As for my mental health, I experience a little dip. I start sending silly letters to Bono again. If they were sane letters, that would be okay, but they are not. Also, around this time, I am having meetings with Nina – who is part of Breakaway; a service connected with Southdown Housing. She suggested that I try voluntary work, as it is a way of learning new skills and gaining confidence. I never really considered it before, but now it seems like a good idea. I decide to make an appointment with the Voluntary Bureau in Crawley. The lady there suggests doing Reflexology at the Olive Tree Cancer Support Centre, at Crawley Hospital.

It sounds so rewarding and it's also nice to find something I actually want to do.

But the dip continues. I listen to U2 too much, and I'm absentminded when I speak to people. The hardest thing to come to terms with, is that I'm not going to come off my medication at all in the future, so I don't have the sanctuary of the Ward to help me. My previous CPN, Mike, told me once that it was much easier to be inside hospital then outside. My new CPN, Miriam, is kind enough, but I hide my dip, fearing that my medication will be increased. I am brilliant at looking well, when I don't feel it.

Around this time, my dad suggests that I take a trip to Montenegro for a few days. I'm not sure how I feel about going on a plane alone, but I agree to go, as I need a break so much. I am also not sure how my dad and I would get on, as I wasn't as well as I could be.

I know that my illness is a form of escapism, but I cannot prevent it. I have some wonderfully vivid dreams as well, but there are also trickster voices that I can't trust.

I cannot always tell the genuine experiences from the false ones. This is the problem with Schizophrenia. There is a side to it that doctors are just not willing to delve into. It's a beautiful illness as well. I know that I am connected with Angels and I'm not afraid of that. Why don't we highlight some of the beautiful things about Schizophrenia? There is a visionary and creative side to it. It's not all bad, you know.

Although I go off track with my life, there is a hidden treasure in all of this: Indy. Every time I go home to my flat he is waiting, and I cuddle him and let him sit on my lap during *Corrie*. I don't know if anyone has ever written about the healing effects of a cat on a person, but I am living proof of this. I receive pure, unconditional love from him.

Indy sparkles with life and never lets me down. Today, nearly half of all households have a cat but there are still so many needing homes. Thank god we have

Cat's Protection and various cat shelters.

One October day, I make my way to Gatwick Airport, feeling spaced out and not looking forward to the flight. Just as I go to board the plane, my mum phones and I tell her that I am okay. I take *Kalms* and, feeling nervous, start my flight. Taking off is my least favourite part of flying. I have a strange fluttering in my heart as we head up, but as we are cruising; I listen to a compilation tape of U2 on my *Walkman*. It takes my mind off of the stress of the flight. In my bag, I also have a notebook with the things that Bono has told me through the night; private things. When I get to Dubrovnik Airport, my dad is waiting for me, looking quite relaxed. It is the first time in a long while that I would be staying him. There is a lengthy drive to Budva , and a ferry trip and, by the time we get to our destination, I am very hungry.

We eat in a nice restaurant on the roadside. I have chicken pieces with potatoes and salad. I am only to stay here 4 nights, but Montenegro is a fascinating place. It is situated in South-Eastern Europe, next to the Adriatic Sea. Croatia is to the west of Montenegro. It is a middle-income country, and on the 21st of May, 2006, it become independent and separated from Serbia.

My dad is renting an apartment on a hilly part of Budva. As I walk in, I notice the tiled floor, and spacious dining area. The kitchen is fitted with a shiny cooker and the beige sofa is in the corner of the living room area. My bedroom is to the left as you walk in, and there is a low double bed; some of my dad's clothes are hanging in an open wardrobe.

The temperature is actually quite cool. I was hoping for more sunshine, but it is October after all. After a restful sleep, we visit Kotor the next day, which is an old town, 30 minutes away. Once there, we have a drink and then my dad sits on his own, while I go wandering around the shops.

I imagine photos being taken of me by the Media. I've always wanted to be famous and my fantasy life can be quite strange at times.

I'm convinced that when I get home and start writing letters, everything will work out perfectly.

In the evening, dad and I watch DVDs and then I retire to my bed to read *Angels In My Hair*, about an Irish mystic who sees Angels. I wish that I saw Angels too, although I definitely do *hear* them sometimes. I get a lot coming in spiritually; the medication doesn't numb me altogether. I guess I'm quite lucky like that. But, the next day, things start to go a little wrong. We go to a restaurant next to a dock and eat a delicious fish meal, and then we sit on the deckchairs. But I'm in a world of my own; not in touch with reality. I can feel myself floating off. Then my dad calls for me: 'Marcia, let's go'.

We are in the car now, and my dad looks agitated. He shouts: 'What's the matter with you? You don't want to do anything. Are you taking your medication?'

'Yes, I am, and I *do* want to do things.'

My dad bellows out: 'Then tell me what you want to do!'

'I don't mind. You are just a bully.'

I can feel tears sting my eyes. My dad drives erratically for a couple of minutes then starts to calm down. My dad doesn't really know how to cope with me, while I'm in this dreamy state. It's strange, because I am taking my medication. I'm not really ill, just a little spaced out. I really wish that I had my mum with me. She always knows how to cope with me.

A little while later, in the apartment, my dad says:

'I'm sorry, Marcia. I just want to make you happy.'

After this, I start to hide my dreamy state and communicate more. The next morning, I find my dad fiddling about with my bed, changing the sheets, and I'm scared in case he has seen my secret notebook. I don't want anyone to see what I've written in my book, as its private.

The next day, we go to Tivet and it is so cold! We have a coffee inside a café with brown leather sofas and a bar. People are smoking inside, which disturbs me, as I breathe in the smoke. Later on, I go and walk on the beach, as the sun glares out through the cold air. My dad takes a picture of me.

The break goes very quickly and, before I know it, I'm going home. I'm looking forward to seeing Indy, who my mum is looking after. My mum meets me at the airport and I tell her about the argument with dad. She says that my dad can't cope with me when I'm not 100%. I'm so glad to see Indy who has grown since I last saw him. I let him jump on my lap and I stroke him tenderly. The following week, I write some silly letters and, of course, get no reply.

Then, suddenly, I stop having dreams and hearing voices and I sleep really well. My delusions are gone, and it's nice to feel well again. I start to concentrate on achieving more realistic goals. The first thing I want to do is phone the Voluntary Bureau about the job; giving Reflexology to cancer patients. A little while later, Marilyn leaves a message asking me to come for an interview. I am really pleased about this.

In the spring, I get involved with a music development company called Major Music, and record my songs with a nice producer. It is based in Farringdon, London and is situated in a basement with three recording studios.

It is wonderful to hear my songs recorded and I'm looking forward to taking part in the upcoming showcases. Going to London once a month gives my life structure and I have to compose a new song, ready for the next recording session.

Music has always been an important part of my life - it's a lovely form of expression. Around this time, I also perform in Brighton at the Brighthelm Church, which is connected to Southdown. I sing two songs with the piano and, although I'm nervous, it goes really well.

It is the first time I've ever performed with the piano and voice and I'm very proud of myself!

Afterwards, a man compares me to Beverly Craven, but I like to think that I have my own unique style.

Not long after that performance, I go to the Olive Tree for my first day at my voluntary job. I am nervous, but kind of excited too. I might meet a new friend - you never know!

Chapter Eleven

New Friends

The Olive Tree is situated in the grounds of Crawley Hospital (it is soon to move to a more spacious area). It's funded by Macmillan Cancer Support and offers many different complementary therapies. The first week there, I work on a therapist and on one of the Trustees too. The next week, I am to practice properly on clients.

My practice builds up and Monday morning proves to be quite busy. I start to love doing it. I give Reflexology to three people in the morning, from a variety of backgrounds. There is a lady who cares for her sick husband and an elderly man mourning for his wife. There are those going through chemo and those recovering from it. It slowly dawns on me that I am lucky in comparison. I have an illness that can be controlled and I can lead a normal life. Cancer is precarious. Even when chemo is finished, there is the threat of it coming back. Another thought dawns on me; people who have suffered, tend to have deep compassion for others. What doesn't kill you makes you stronger. I did go through a very hard time when I was ill, but my illness is not life threatening. I like listening to all of the client's stories and I have a compassionate ear.

On my birthday, I am in Montenegro again, soaking up the sun. I sip wine in a beautiful restaurant and eat paella. My dad takes me to all of the familiar haunts: Kotor and Sveti Stefan etc. It is not that hot, but I swim in the sea everyday, anyway. I really enjoy the present moment and the feeling of being really well. My dad is kind to me and I have a lovely time. I do not want to go home at all – I have such a lovely rest.

Two months later, I go to a U2 concert at Wembley Stadium. Bono is as charming as ever and tells the audience that we have a beautiful country. They are doing a world tour and we are lucky to see them. My mum and I get really carried away and clap throughout the concert. At one point, Bono seemed to look my way, and I smiled at him, for what seemed like ages. I know it seems like a fantasy, but I could feel his glare through my soul. He reminds me a little of Elvis. He has got an amazing charisma and yet this real innocence in his heart. Everyone has their own opinion of him, and I'm sure he is not perfect, but there's something in him that I almost want to mother. I remember that I had a picture of him on my dormitory wall, in the Ward, and a nurse asked me who the dishy guy was!

Well he is *dishy,* but there is also something special about him, and there's also all of the good work he does for poverty and the Third World. He wouldn't bother doing that unless he really cared. I think that he is one of the kindest people on the planet. And as for U2 they are an amazing band live, and the music can really reach into the depths of your soul. The claw-like stage was interesting too. I can't help but write a letter to them, saying how much I love their concert.

The prayers in my heart, at the psychiatric ward, all centred round U2. Their music got me through many a dull day, and all I can say is - you never know what the future might hold. Who knows what is around the corner!

Around this time, I am discharged from my psychiatrist, as I am doing very well.

I still take medication and I have a support worker that helps me every two weeks.

One day, I decided to go for a walk around Tilgate Park and I bumped into my old friend Rebecca and her two children.

'Hello, Marcia, is that you?' Rebecca said.

'Hi... Rebecca! Oh my god!'

We embrace, as we haven't seen each other for a long time.

'These are my children.'

A beautiful little girl and a gorgeous baby boy.

'I can't believe it, Rebecca! ' I said.

'Nor can I!' Rebecca replies. 'What are you doing at the moment?'

'I give Reflexology at the Hospital.'

'It's so weird, us bumping into one another like this! How long has it been?' Rebecca asks.

'It's been a long time. I added you on *Facebook*. Are you still with Ricky?'

'Yes, I am.' Rebecca replies.

'Where do you live?'

'In Cuckfield – and you must come to visit.'

'I'd love to visit.' I reply.

'How is your music going?'

'I'm with a music development company now.'

'That sounds good.' Rebecca says,

'Do you have any friends, Rebecca?'

'I don't have any!'

'Neither do I!'

'Aren't we both so sad!' Rebecca laughs.

'Yes!'

'Let's make a promise to meet at least once a month.'

'That would be great!' I say, happily.

I can't describe how wonderful it is to meet up with Rebecca. I needed a friend so much. She is kind and supportive and my only friend.

When I mention her to my mum, she says how nice it is to get to know her children as well.

Two weeks later, I visit her house in Cuckfield. She lives in a terraced cottage with a very homely feel. Rebecca and I can talk for hours about all manner of things - it's strange how a friendship can open your heart again. Around this time, I also make friends with a client of mine, called Coran. Both of my friends are born under the sign of Cancer, just like me, and they each are very sensitive. They are wonderful friends. Everyone needs friends and I need them too. They both came into my life at the right time and blessed my life with their presence. Friends can be more objective about things and offer advice. I no longer need to be in a psychiatric ward to find them. They are a reality in my life.

Another wonderful experience is getting involved in Music again. My producer is really nice and supportive and eventually I ended up performing in a summer showcase.

It was a hot, sticky day and I wore my floral summer dress in the packed bar, close to Covent Garden. As I took to the stage, I panicked and almost fainted from the heat, but then my fingers touched the keyboard and I started to sing: *December*, a self-composed song. I get a great response and afterwards join my mother. Like all proud mums she says that I was the most unique performer there.

It is a similar experience at Xmas, when I perform without a piano - a lot of performers don't turn up, because of the snow. I wish everyone a Merry Christmas, then start singing: *Strange Kind Of Girl*.

My style is quite different to the rest, but I love the experience of being on stage. It's not all about being famous. I'm dressed in black, with a long, black lace skirt. I'm brimming with positivity - and my heart feels open.

On Boxing Day, I visit Rebecca's house and give presents to both of her children. I buy her son a Jack-in-the-box, and give her daughter a soft polar bear, and some books.

I'm soon to find out that I will be a godparent to her son. It's so nice to have somewhere else to visit and to have such a lovely friend in Rebecca. I often think that it was like divine intervention, us meeting in the park that day. It was predestined. Rebecca is like an older sister to me and we have an uncanny way of helping each other.

I need help in February, as my Nan dies, after being in a nursing home for seven years. My mum and I often visited her. I am upset about this, until I have a dream that she is young again and saying goodbye to me. My Nan had become institutionalised in the Home. It's sad when that happens. Time must have gone very slowly for her. Now she is free spiritually, and, as far as I'm concerned, she is in Heaven and with my granddad. They are probably arguing! She had a low-key funeral at the crematorium and then a gathering at my brother's house. We all got out old photographs and reminisced about the past.

As for me, life is going really well. I enjoy my voluntary work, and spending time with friends and I'm generally very busy all of the time.

Summer soon arrives and my birthday has come around again. Rebecca and I are a day apart - with her birthday on the 23rd and mine on the 24th of June.

My dad buys tickets for us to *Billy Elliot*, and it is absolutely brilliant. We laugh our socks off. Then, afterwards, we go to Covent Garden and sit outside, eating a meal. We get talking to two Dutch guys who are highly intellectual and too young for us! But we have a great night and plan our early escape.

On the train home, I am tipsy from the wine and Rebecca and I have a spat. But, the next day, we make it up and laugh about it.

In September, I go to Montenegro with my mum and we stay in a 4-star hotel in Budva. It is so hot that I nearly faint, but we have a really good time, playing cards and swimming in the pool.

I experience quite bad pre-menstrual tension, and, when I am in Tivet, I experience my first panic attack in a very long time. I used to get them when I was in a psychotic state, before I went to hospital. It is not the voices that are hard to deal with for me, but the panic attacks. My throat becomes very tight, and I can't breathe and I almost start hitting myself. It's a really unpleasant feeling and almost a feeling like you are going to die from panic. While I am in Tivet, I am dehydrated and my dad goes to find water, but can't find any, so this panics me even more. It's a shame to be on holiday and feel unwell.

When I come home, I have to visit the doctor, as I start to have panic attacks daily. Even going out becomes a problem. The doctor doubles my medication and it seems to help, but I still experience a tight throat.

I know not everyone believes in spiritual things, but I feel the only thing I can do with these panic attacks is to start to pray for help. Miraculously, this does work and I bring my dose down to 7.5 mg and slowly, but surely, start to feel better again; once more I experience the normality of life.

The most important things with panic attacks are to push through them and force yourself to go out and do things. This, in fact, helps with all forms of mental illness. Thinking positive is very important and pushing through anxiety works. Each time you go out, it gets easier.

I experience another shock to the system.

My other grandmother dies at the age of 87. The day before, I find a large white feather and believe this is a sign of her saying *goodbye* to me.

The funeral is held in a small church with an elderly woman playing *Amazing Grace* on the piano. My grandmother is buried next to my granddad, who died 17 years ago. It just makes me aware of the fragility of life and how we must value every single moment of it. Life is precious indeed.

Around this time, something surprising happens to me. I have a dream that I should write about my mental health experiences and that I will be a literary artist. Like the Reflexology dream, I had before; it is very vivid and uplifting. I have an idea to get my book copy-edited by a literary consultant. There aren't many books about Schizophrenia from the viewpoint of someone who has had it, and I believe that my story would give hope to others.

It is a story of how I have survived a mental illness and have come out of the other side.

The story of a girl who writes to U2, creates songs, gives Reflexology and has a cat and her own beautiful flat.

Quickly, I start scribbling away, as my memories come back to me.

And it all ends with this next chapter.

It all ends with Grace.

Chapter Twelve

Grace

So... this is the last chapter.

I have been in the murkiest of waters and survived. I have plunged down to the depths of the ocean and I have scaled the tallest mountain.

Nothing bothers me now.

I have friends; I go out for coffee with Coran, catch a gig with Eve or go to Rebecca's house. I work part time and get tax credits. I do voluntary work and I've just finished doing a massage course at College.

I've recorded songs with a good producer, and sometimes I perform at small venues. I'm hoping to do more with my music in the future; I want to perform a lot more too.

I put this book on hold for a long time and then a strange thing happened. I was in a bookstore and I found a book about a homeless man who befriends a stray cat called Bob (it is called: A Street Cat Named Bob, by James Bowen) and it details the story of how he gets over drug addiction. This educated me about drug addiction, and it gave me hope. It made me realise that there must be a way of my story being told and understood.

I want to change people's perceptions of mental illness. I want to show how I have totally rebuilt my life and offer hope to others.

I am always busy in my life. I think that life is precious and I want to enjoy every moment. I have discovered also that I love to write... maybe there is another book in me!

I love the song *Grace* by U2 and I have based my book around this song. When nothing makes sense that is my favourite word.

Grace will lift you up one day. It will take away the aches and pains, and awaken you to your true life's destiny. It's in every single person you meet and in the places that you go to.

Grace awakens your intuition and will never let you down.

There are too many stories of people with mental illness being dangerous and causing havoc around them. There are many people with mental illness who are gentle and need to be treated with compassion. We need to not judge them and to encourage them to live their dreams. I have vivid dreams and hear voices, but I live a totally normal life. I have never been nasty or cruel; I wrote my songs and penned letters to U2... and I painted flowers.

The hardest thing for me to come to terms with, is the medication. But, the truth is, I cannot sleep without it. I don't want to go back to the panic attacks - I want to live a normal life. I know the reality is that I have to stay on this medication for the rest of my life. It's something I have now come to terms with and I will tell you why: I see mental illness as a gift. It can make you grow if you let it.

Rebecca said that I could help a lot of people, in the future. I feel that she is right.

Those with mental illness should not waste their lives being in and out of hospital. It's best just to stay on the medication. They need to have meaning to their lives and they need to be positive.

I have discovered that I love touch therapies like Reflexology and massage, writing and music.

The advice from me is to do what you love. Don't let your mental illness get in the way. Don't use it as an excuse not to live your life.

Live life to the full and be happy.

Everything is relative. When I was locked in a ward I felt enclosed and my sense of freedom was lost. Now I marvel at the beautiful flat I have and my dear cat Indy. I am always active in my life and I make sure that I exercise twice a week. I am grateful to all of the lovely nurses who looked after me when I was ill, and to the psychiatrists too. I only wish that they would be more open minded about mental illness as being a path towards spirituality, and psychic experiences. No medication can take away this gift I have. I believe in Angels and know that they exist. They are a natural part of my life.

Why is mental illness controversial? Why is there a stigma? I don't know the answer to these questions. Perhaps this is the time when perceptions of mental illness are starting to change. We should be able to be honest about our mental illnesses.

I totally live a normal life. If people are narrow minded, that is not my problem.

I pray and meditate and always focus on the positive.

The stigma used to be cancer, but now it is mental illness. This simply has to change. The way I paint the world, it is full of bright colours and hope. I have a beautiful mind but, more importantly, I have a beautiful heart.

Suffering allows us to grow and mature. In the end, it brings out the best in us, and makes us more compassionate.

People with mental illness want your understanding. Many are gifted and should focus on this. The stigma has to go, and I hope that my book will help with that. Let us bless mental illness, and everyone who has it.

It is definitely possible to turn your life around, once you've had mental illness. I still have a choice about how to live my life and I don't need to be hard on myself anymore.

What keeps me sane is that word *Grace*. I listen to that U2 song every day. Mental illness is a *Journey Through Grace*. It is a blessing in disguise. Every moment of my life has been so full of Grace that I almost want to cry.

I wake up in the morning and I live in gratitude for the day ahead. I am so lucky to have survived this mental illness and to be treated with the utmost care by medical staff, family and friends.

This has led me to a total and utter state of Grace, for now and forever more.

5635529R

Printed in Great Britain
by Amazon.co.uk, Ltd.,
Marston Gate.